Riding the Tiger's Tail

Gary Giamboi

ISBN: 0692296697

ISBN 13: 9780692296691

Table of Contents

Foreword

Summer time in Japan 2014:

I am very happy to publish this great book by my one of the top students in USA, Kyoshi Gary Giamboi.

Kyoshi Giamboi has followed me for many years (from 1990) as my personal student and opened his martial arts school (Dojo) to introduce and offer guidance in true traditional Japanese martial arts through me.

Kyoshi Giamboi is very gentle person and really patient person for any hard training and hard teaching. He has never given up and still continues to follow me to this day.

This book is the story of how the Genbukan/KJJR developed and came to be known in New York, USA area. It contains many stories and episodes you won't read about anywhere else.

I would like to say: Thank you very much to everyone who has remained our member. I pray for our members, for those who have left us and, indeed, for all people to be successful as a True Human Being.

Sincerely Yours,

— *Shoto Tanemura*

種 村 匠 刀 流 派 相 伝 一 覧 表
SHOTO TANEMURA GRANDMASTERSHIPS & MENKYO KAIDEN LIST

玄武館世界忍法武芸連盟会長（Genbukan World Ninpo Bugei Federation President）
国際柔術連盟会長（Kokusai Jujutsu Renmei Federation President）
日本古流武術世界連盟会長（Japan Koryu Bujutsu World Federation President）

天津鞴韜武門宗門第五十八代宗家(Amatsu Tatara Bumon & Shumon 58th Soke)
神伝鞴韜流體術第五十五代宗家(Shinden Tatara Ryu Taijutsu 55th Soke)
神伝馗韜流棒術第五十五代宗家(Shinden Kito Ryu Bojutsu 55th Soke)
本體楊心高木流柔術第十八代宗家(Hontai Yoshin Takagi Ryu Jujutsu 18th Soke)
本體九鬼神流棒術第十八代宗家(Hontai Kukishin Ryu Bojutsu 18th Soke)
天眞兵法九鬼神流第十八代宗家(Tenshin Hyoho Kukishin-Ryu 18th Soke)
義鑑流骨法術第十四代宗家（Gikan Ryu Koppo-Jutsu 14th Soke）
浅山一傳流体術第十八代宗家（Asayama Ichiden Ryu Taijutsu 18th Soke）
中国拳法八卦掌第五世伝人(Chinese Martial Art Hakkesho 5th Denjin)
卜傳流柔術免許皆伝（Bokuden Ryu Jujutsu Menkyo Kaiden）
天心古流拳法免許皆伝　（Tenshin Ko-Ryu Kenpo Menkyo Kaiden）
一天柳心冑介流柔術免許皆伝（Itten Ryushin Chukai Ryu Jujutsu Menkyo Kaiden）
荒木新流柔術免許皆伝（Araki Shin Ryu Menkyo Kaiden）
柳生心眼流兵法甲冑柔免許皆伝（Yagyu Shingan Kacchu Yawara Menkyo Kaiden）
神伝不動流打拳体術免許皆伝（Shinden Fudo Ryu Daken Taijutsu Menkyo Kaiden）
九鬼神伝八方秘剣術免許皆伝（Kukishinden Happo Biken-Jutsu Menkyo Kaiden）
戸隠流忍法免許皆伝（Togakure Ryu Ninpo Menkyo Kaiden）
玉虎流骨指術免許皆伝(Gyokko Ryu Kosshi-Jutsu Menkyo Kaiden)
虎倒流骨法術免許皆伝（Koto Ryu Koppo-Jutsu Menkyo Kaiden）
馗神澄水流打拳體術免許皆伝（Kijin Chosui Ryu Daken-Taijutsu Menkyo Kaiden）
大東流合気柔術免許皆伝（Daito Ryu Aiki Jujutsu Yamamoto-Ha Menkyo Kaiden）
無限神刀流居合術免許皆伝（Mugen Shinto Ryu Iai-jutsu Menkyo Kaiden）

Preface

Before you begin to read this book, I would like to briefly explain to you a few points about my style of writing.

First, when I refer to Shoto Tanemura in a context where he is my *Sensei* (instructor) and the passage relates to me, I refer to him as Tanemura *Sensei*. When I refer to him more generally as he relates to people other than myself, I refer to him as Tanemura *Soke* (Grandmaster).

Secondly, when I wish to emphasize a word, I will capitalize it for the same reason I would put more emphasis on it as if I was speaking directly to you.

By doing this, I hope to make it clear which points I believe are more important than others and not leave it to the reader to guess for themselves.

For the sake of readability and traditional English grammar, and not because of any gender bias, I have used the masculine pronouns most of the time. Where I thought it would not get in the way of a thought's flow, I used both the masculine and feminine forms of pronouns.

If a person were to hold on very tightly to a larger creature which was traveling somewhere, whose journey would it be?

Would it be only the journey of the larger creature which was physically performing the actions of traveling or would the person holding on to the moving creature also have his own unique journey?

Think about it.

Let's assume the moving entity is a Tiger and the rider is holding on to its tail.

Wouldn't the Tiger always see things ahead more clearly, decide where to go, how fast to go, when to stop, always arrive first and receive the credit for making the journey possible?

Wouldn't the rider be able to travel faster and further holding on to The Tiger's tail than if he attempted to make the journey on their own?

Of course these attributes make it seem as if it is absolutely better for everyone to be The Tiger and perhaps it is.

However, let us not forget The Tiger has much greater responsibility.

He must decide which journey to take, make all of the critical decisions necessary to arrive safely, battle stronger head winds, fight any enemies that appear along the way and finally, once the destination was reached, he must determine whether or not it he should remain there.

The rider may not get as much glory and fame as The Tiger does (perhaps even none); but he would be just a step or two behind the Tiger and get to see things from a different prospective than the Tiger.

The rider may even get to see things along the way that the Tiger could not see. And the rider does not have to expend as much energy as The Tiger does in order to reach his destination.

These are just some of the obvious benefits and drawbacks to being in either position.

However, there are other factors which must be taken into account:

Not everyone is or can be a Tiger; and, not every Tiger can complete his journey without some help along the way.

The bottom line is:

It is only better for Tigers to be Tigers; and for everyone else to be only What They Truly Are.

Riding a Tiger's Tail as a method of travel is not suitable for everyone, Tigers and non-Tigers alike. Some of us are simply more suited to traveling our paths alone or in larger groups.

The Rider has to trust in The Tiger's Wisdom.

The Rider has to believe because he knows who The Tiger is; he can know where the Tiger is heading.

What if the Tiger was heading to "a Tiger picnic" where every attending Tiger was supposed to bring something for the other Tigers to eat?

Actually, it is very hard for the rider to know exactly where the Tiger will end up.

So how can I say the rider has to Trust where The Tiger is taking him when he doesn't know exactly where The Tiger is heading?

I mean we have to Trust that The Tiger is heading some place that will be good for us even if we do not know the exact nature or location of that place.

Do children know the nature and location of where their parents are taking them every time they get into the car with them?

No, of course they do not. They simply trust their parents' won't do anything that will be harmful to them.

Actually, it is even more complicated than it seems.

Even if somehow the rider can find out where The Tiger is heading when he first grabs his tail, how can the rider be sure The Tiger won't change his mind along the way?

It is also difficult for The Tiger to decide to allow a rider to hitch a ride with him.

Why?

Perhaps you are wondering what a powerful Tiger has to worry about from an insignificant little rider.

Actually, he can have a lot to lose.

I am sure most of us know there are animal names for each of the twelve years in the Chinese Lunar calendar.

Here's the story about how those twelve years acquired their animal names:

It seems the Buddha summoned all the animals to come to him and bid him farewell before his Spirit left his body.

Only twelve animals heeded his call. As a reward he named one year of the cycle after each animal that came to him in the order they actually appeared before him.

It so happens that of the twelve animals, the OX traveled the quickest; and the shrewd little Rat knew this. So the Rat asked the not overly bright OX to let him hitch a ride on his back.

The easy-going Ox agreed because the Rat explained his legs were so short he would never arrive in time.

However, when the OX was just about to arrive first, the Rat jumped off his back and sprinted up to The Buddha and arrived first.

As a reward, The Buddha named the first year in the 12 year cycle after The Rat.

And so it remains to this day that The OX lost the glory of being the first of the Twelve Animals.

Therefore, both the Rider and the Tiger have to know and trust each other's values and sense of honor.

If they agree to share some of the duties and responsibilities they know they will encounter along the way, then they have to have trust in each other's abilities and sense of duty as well. Otherwise, there may be an unexpected, serious consequence to a seemingly simple arrangement.

You can see there has to be a bond between the rider and the Tiger. The stronger the bond, the more likely the rider will look out for the Tiger and the Tiger will take care of the rider.

The Tiger may let a more trusted rider ride closer to his body, perhaps even on his back; while a less trusted rider will be relegated towards the tip of his tail. The closer to the Tiger's center a rider is positioned, the easier and the safer it is for both of them.

If an instructor has a mission and a purpose, both the instructor and his students must take that into account when deciding whether or not to ask and accept each other.

A wrong student may slow an instructor down or even keep him from reaching his goal.

A wrong instructor may drag his student into a situation the student does not wish to be in or show him things he does not want to know and not show him things he does wish to learn.

Although it is important for both Tiger and rider to make the right choices, I believe it is more important for the student to choose the right instructor than for the instructor to choose the right student.

Why?

Because while it is true the Rat out foxed the OX, probability says in most cases a Tiger will find a way to fight for and get to where he is going regardless of what his little rider attempts to do.

While the little rat can travel only as far as its little legs will take him and can only see what he can see from a few inches above the ground.

Tanemura *Sensei* asked me to lunch a few days after I arrived at the *Honbu Dojo* for training in July, 2013.

As usual, he went out of his way to take me to a very nice place which would accommodate my being a lacto-vegetarian.

As we left his car and started walking to the restaurant, Tanemura *Sensei* asked me: "How long have you been with me?"

Notice he didn't say "How long have you been training with me."

Asking the question in this way was actually a very high compliment to me as a person.

Tanemura *Sensei* was showing me that he believed our relationship was more than just that of an instructor for hire with his paying student.

He was telling me each of us had accepted the other in the role of *Koryu* (Traditional or Old School Japanese Martial Art) *Sensei* and his *Deshi* (student).

I replied I was at the *Taikai* as a student of my former instructor the year Tanemura *Sensei* trained the Nassau County Police Department for the first time: 1988. So it has been twenty-five years.

Even though this particular restaurant is located in an out of the way location, its food is so good we had to wait fifteen minutes for a table. During this time, we spoke about how my friends in the Genbukan were doing. *Sensei* made it a point to tell me how impressed he was with UK *Dojo-Cho* Stuart Allison's approximately five hundred students.

Then, we were seated in a private room in a restaurant which serves completely natural, and sometimes organic, local Japanese cuisine. Its specialty is homemade stoneground soba noodles.

Once we settled in, Tanemura *Sensei* and I spoke about the changes in our lives since last year; thus bringing each other up to date with ourselves. After some time, in keeping with his usual practice at these welcome lunches, *Sensei* asked me what I would like to study while I was there.

I mentioned some things I had been working on for a couple of years: *Nanadan Taijutsu, Nanadan Jujutsu and Shodan Naginata Jutsu.*

Sensei agreed with my request; and he added without my saying anything: "I will test you the next time you come to *Honbu*."

Because I train at *Honbu* at least once a year, we both knew this meant next year.

I sincerely thanked my *Sensei* very much.

We talked a little bit more and then without warning, Tanemura *Sensei* hit me right between the eyes when he said:

"So you have been with me twenty-five years.

Why have you stayed with me for so long"?

In today's world, it is not usual for a student to stay with the same teacher for so long. Therefore, Tanemura *Sensei* now wanted to know why I stayed by his side for twenty-five years.

This is a much more personal question.

It is based upon a true two-way personal relationship; and not upon what one person is getting from the other person.

Reflecting back, I see I did not hesitate. I simply said "Because of you, Sensei."

Then I related to Tanemura *Sensei* the following true story:

As a Martial Arts teacher, people are always asking me the following question:

"I always wanted to study a Martial Art or my child wants to study karate, but I don't know what style to choose. What do you think"?

I always say to them:

"You will be much better off in the long run if you choose the best teacher for yourself or your child instead of choosing the style."

Suddenly, *Sensei* cut me off by saying:

"Exactly!

I would like you to write a book about me so people can understand this point. This is most important."

And so, here we are.

This is my story about my instructor's rise to World Fame (as seen through my eyes) and the journey which has led me to earn a *Nanadan* (7th Degree Black Belt) in the *Kokusai Jujutsu Renmei*, which is a True *Koryu Jujutsu*.

In Japanese, *Koryu* means traditional or old-school.

Some parts of this story may seem so tied into other parts of this story that it may seem as if I made them up just so everything fit together as nicely as it does.

However, the truth is:

Everything has unfolded just as I am about to relate it.

Chapter 1:
The Beginning

I began my martial art journey in 1969.

Looking back, I see this is true even though at the time, I was unaware I was doing anything more than trying to learn how to be like Bruce Lee.

A friend of mine told me he had heard of a very good karate instructor on Avenue U in Brooklyn; and we had to go there to find out what it was all about.

We did.

I became a student who stayed for several years. He left after a short while.

I am not sure when I first discovered that I believed in *Ki* (*Qi* in Chinese), the Universal Cosmic Energy that powers everything in Creation. But once I did, I came to realize this was the first giant step on My Path.

The next momentous milestone on My Path occurred when I realized if I was connected to the One Universal Energy Source, then so was everybody and everything else. That, in turn, made me realize I was connected to All of Creation.

I didn't know it at that time; but, this understanding altered the course of my life.

OK. That's not correct.

Although I said that last statement as many people would; it is not true.

I should have said: that realization made me aware I needed to change the path my life was on.

There is an old Chinese adage I like:

If you don't change the road you are on, you will end up where it is headed.

And so, this new understanding forced me to alter the direction I was traveling; and it set The Path my life would take. It has possibly even determined my final destination.

I have come to believe the purpose of my life is for me to Fully realize what it means to be connected to Everything else.

I know this is not a life's purpose that will gain me great fame and wealth. However, it will gain me what I have come to hold higher than everything else:

The Truth of The Way Things Truly Are.

Of course, My Path has become more and more refined as I have spent more time with it.

Did you notice I did not say "as I spent more time traveling on it." There is an extremely important concept which governs why I chose the words I did.

It is this concept:

Once you are Fully on your life's True Path, The True Path Takes You. You do not take it.

There is an old saying:

Fate leads those that follow it; and drags those who don't.

My personal view point is if I am going to get there eventually one way or the other, I might as well try to minimize the amount of kicking, screaming and weeping-and-gnashing of teeth I will do along The Way.

OK. OK. This is not completely true either. But, I wanted to ease you into what I believe to be The Truth.

The only way to truly follow your life's True Path is to allow yourself to Become The Path.

That's Right.

If there is no difference between You and Your Path, then You and The Path are The Same.

If there is a difference between You and Your Path, then you cannot be following Your Path Exactly or with Full Belief in All that unfolds while you are on it.

When I see Tanemura *Soke*, I do not see a person who says he believes in *Amatsu Tatara* (*Amatsu Tatara* is the Highest Secret Teachings of Heaven's Way for Shumon or Spiritual Philosophy and Bumon or Martial Techniques and Philosophy).

Instead, I see *Amatsu Tatara* alive and living through, with, in and By Tanemura *Soke*, who is the 58th Grandmaster of *Amatsu Tatara*.

When I see Tanemura *Soke*, I do not see a person who practices *Koryu* (traditional) Martial Arts. I see a Martial Artist whose Martial Arts animate his spirit as surely as his breathing animates his body.

It is That Simple.

However, as I said in my first book, *The Spirit of Smiling: Perfecting The Art of Surrendering to The Way:*

"Simple" does not mean easy.

In fact, "Simple" things are usually more difficult to do outstandingly well than more complex ones.

Ancient cultures knew this when they chose the word for what we call in English a "teacher" or an "instructor." In particular, I want to discuss the Japanese word which they use instead of "teacher": *Sensei.*

In Japanese, *Sensei* means:

"He who has gone before."

This meaning is especially poignant when one is discussing Recognizing, Choosing, Following and Becoming One with your life's True Path.

The fact a *Sensei* has traveled that same path or a similar path before others have done so makes him able to share his personal knowledge with those people in a way only his personal experiences make possible.

Of course, nothing enables complete understanding better than your own personal experience.

However, most people will sacrifice some of the personal understanding of what it is like to fall off a cliff and get smashed on the rocks below in order to be better able to complete their life's journey.

Actually, this particular point is exactly the one which separates a good *Sensei* from one not as good.

A good *Sensei* will have an understanding of which concepts no student should have to experience personally, which concepts all students should experience and which ones some students should and other students should not experience.

At this point in this book, for obvious reasons, I would like to use the Japanese word, *Sensei,* in place of the English word, "teacher."

This brings us back to the previous point of a *Sensei's* and his student's mutual knowledge of each other.

The better a *Sensei* knows his student, the better able he is to choose which experiences his student needs to experience personally.

The better a student knows his *Sensei,* the more he will trust his *Sensei's* judgment in these matters.

As you can see, there is supposed to be a lot of personal contact between a *Sensei* and his student. Indeed, the first test a student must pass is to be accepted as student who is permitted to have direct personal contact with the *Sensei.*

The titles of *Renshi* (1st level of mastership), *Kyoshi* (2nd level of mastership), *Jun-Shihan* (3rd level of mastership), *Shihan* (4th level of mastership) and *Shibucho* (regional director) are much more than a measure of someone's physical abilities. They are a measure of the student's acceptance as a personal student by Tanemura *Soke.*

This means these titles are actually a measure of Tanemura *Soke's* trust in the student's acceptance of Tanemura *Soke* as his *Sensei.*

First comes the acceptance by the student; and then comes the acknowledgment by the *Sensei.*

For the Genbukan, this means Tanemura *Soke* defines the role of *Sensei.*

The student does not define the role of *Sensei.*

If the student defines the role of his *Sensei,* then the student is telling the *Sensei* what his role, his job and his worth is.

Doesn't that seem strange to you?

Personally, I would never accept a *Sensei* who would accept that position.

What is the purpose of seeking out someone who "has gone before" you and traveled the path you now want to travel just to tell him:

"Only tell me what I want to hear when I want to hear it"?

Obviously, if the *Sensei* defines his personal role, then it follows that he must also define the role of his *deshi* or student.

This is the essence of what separates traditional students from modern students.

Modern students tend to treat their instructors like shop keepers: people who have something to sell for money.

This means as long as a student has the money, he can buy whatever it is he wishes to learn.

In a traditional Japanese school headed by a traditional *Sensei* of a traditional Japanese subject matter or art, money couldn't even buy your way Into the school, much less be the only thing you needed to give to that *Sensei.*

The student needed to do or give to the *Sensei* whatever it was he was required to by the *Sensei*.

Now that I have explained some of the concepts this book is based upon, I can begin.

The following is the story of my *Sensei*'s rise to the top of his world and into the world's top tier of martial artists as viewed by me while holding on to his tail.

Chapter 2:
My Early
Genbukan Years

I met Tanemura *Soke* for the first time in New York 1988. He had been invited by my former instructor to give a seminar to demonstrate true Ninpo.

It was a big seminar with over two hundred attendees.

I remember it was held in a gymnasium in Nassau County, New York. There were no mats; so we practiced *kaiten* (rolling) on the hard wood floors from one end of the gym to the other for what seemed like forever.

We did fifty repetitions on each side of every *kihon* (the standard, basic variation of a technique) *uke and atemi* (blocking and striking)...except for *suwari tsuki* (Dropping down to half kneeling and punching). *Soke* said he would be kind to us and only require us to do twenty five repetitions on each side.

This was perhaps the most physically demanding *Taikai* I have ever attended.

Tanemura *Soke* was younger and less forgiving of physical weakness in those days. He knew firsthand if his students wanted

"To Defend Well; they would have to Train Hard."

Tanemura *Soke* was prepared to make sure his student's trained hard. Anyone who couldn't endure this kind of training was free to leave.

Tanemura *Soke* never planned on sacrificing quality for quantity.

For as long as Tanemura *Sensei* and I had conversations about the Genbukan, he always told me he was willing to accept never having a large following as long as his *Senseis* would be proud of the students he did have.

Soke also realized in order to fulfill his mission of preserving and sharing Takamatsu, Kimura and Sato Senseis' Original *Koryu* Martial Training Methods and *Koryu* Spiritual Way with the world, he would have to be very patient. He would have to persevere for as long as it would take the world to recognize The Truth of these teachings.

However, that did not stop Tanemura *Soke* from moving forward with his plan.

He planned and made well thought out, strategic moves.

Just like Japanese Industry, Tanemura *Soke* was willing to sacrifice short term gains in order to sow special seeds which would give abundant fruit If they were given enough time and care to mature properly.

Like any warrior, *Soke* always put attaining his goal of bringing true Japanese *Koryu* Martial Arts to the world ahead of his personal feelings as long as no harm was done to anyone except himself.

Tanemura *Soke* never wanted other people to make sacrifices for his dream.

However, this is not as simple a statement as it seems.

Why?

Because how can a *Sensei*'s goal be completely unimportant to a close personal student?

Indeed, one measure of the closeness of a Traditional *Sensei-Deshi* (Instructor-Student) relationship is how closely their goals and plans are related to each other.

Tanemura *Soke* understands how most people think and feel.

He knows that many people misunderstand what it means to study a *Koryu* Japanese Art under a *Koryu Sensei*.

He knows that most people would say they want to learn a *Koryu* Japanese art because they are the arts whose value has been proven on a battlefield or in to-the-death personal combat.

Yet, most of those same people think it is possible to learn a traditional art without forming a traditional *Sensei-Deshi* (teacher-student) relationship.

The traditional Japanese *Sensei-Deshi* relationship was designed not only to teach a person how to defend themselves; but, to mold a Martial Art Student's Spirit into that of a True *Samurai's* Spirit.

In fact, some *Senseis* would consider the later more important than the former.

Most people accept the fact each of us has an upper limit to our physical abilities which we will not be able to surpass (unless we master the art of using *Ki*; and even then, there is a limit to what would be possible).

However, how many people accept a limit on how Pure their Heart and Spirit can become?

Does each of us have an upper limit on Our Goodness in the same the way we have with a limit to our muscular strength and endurance?

I don't think so.

Chapter 3:
More of The Early Years

In the late 1980's, I became a student of a *Jujutsu* instructor who had attended a seminar given by Tanemura *Soke* in the Mid-West of the USA. Not long after that, my former instructor decided to invite Tanemura *Soke* to give a *Taikai* in New York.

At some point just before, during or after that seminar, my instructor joined the Genbukan.

In those early days, Tanemura *Soke* allowed *Dojo-cho* (black belts who owned martial art schools) to join the Genbukan World Ninpo Federation (GWNBF) and keep their status as *Dojo-cho*. In certain cases, he also allowed them to wear their black belts out of respect to their previous practices.

This was how I began to learn the Genbukan Martial Arts while I continued to study my former instructor's American *goshinjutsu* (self-defense techniques).

He was a good martial artist; and his system worked. However, when I saw a True *Koryu* Martial Art performed by a True *Koryu Soke*, I realized I had Never seen True Martial Arts before this.

Tanemura *Soke's Taijutsu and Jujutsu* were simply breath-taking.

Soke moved like no one I had ever seen before.

His techniques burst forth from his *kamaes* (fighting stances) like the sun bursts forth from behind swift moving clouds.

I was especially taken with Tanemura *Soke's Kenjutsu* (sword fighting techniques).

In the late 1980's and early 1990's, I was not married; and I had some money to spend. I am sure this is one of the reasons why my martial arts instructor invited me to attend a New York Met's baseball game with just himself and Tanemura *Soke* during the time of the first New York *Taikai*.

I sat next to *Soke* during the game. That was the first time we got to know a little about each other. It was also the first time I socialized with a Japanese national.

Not realizing that Western pop culture was already greatly influencing Japan, I exhibited a little too much enthusiasm in explaining everything that was happening in the stadium (the music, the food vendors, the behavior of the fans, etc).

I'll never forget the instance when they started playing *The Banana Boat Song* by Harry Belafonte in the stadium. I became too enthusiastic explaining the who, what, when and where of the song to *Soke*.

After he patiently waited for me to finish what-now-seems-like a rather long winded, slightly condescending tale, *Soke* turned to me and said: "Yes, this song is very popular in Japan too" using a tone which politely let me know I was being condescending.

Having realized my mistake, I felt foolish; but, I was extremely impressed with how Tanemura *Soke* handled the situation. There was no evidence of "putting me in my place." He adroitly let me put myself in my place by simply telling me Japan and, by extension, he were as contemporary as I was.

After that initial meeting, I had no special contact with Tanemura *Soke* until one of his subsequent New York *Taikais* to which he brought his instructor, Sato Kinbei *Sensei* and his daughter, with him.

They demonstrated a lot of Chinese Martial Arts at that *Taikai*; and I was very impressed with the *Baguazhang* and *Qigong* I saw. So I asked my former instructor if we could ask Tanemura *Sensei* if I could study the Chinese Arts with Sato Kinbei *Sensei*.

After receiving my former instructor's permission, I asked Tanemura *Soke* for his permission. *Soke* looked directly into my eyes and asked me "Who is your instructor"?

I replied to him "you are." He then looked me straight in the eye once more, turned around and walked away.

The conversation ended there.

It was up to me to realize I had answered my own question.

During my first trip Japan to train at the *Honbu Dojo* (the main Dojo in the Genbukan which was Tanemura *Soke's* dojo) in 1990, I trained again in *Qigong* and Chinese Martial Arts.

While still in Japan, I asked Tanemura *Soke* if I could have permission to study *Baguazhang* in New York. This time, he said yes.

I searched all over New York, including Chinatown, for almost one year for an instructor I wanted to train with. I gave up on *Baguazhang* and considered learning *Taijiquan* (Tai Chi).

Just then, a friend of mine who was learning *Lama Pai Gung Fu* from an old traditional Chinese *Sifu* (master in Chinese) told me a martial art friend of his *Sifu* had just arrived from southern China and is teaching *Taijiquan* in Chinatown.

His instructor thought so highly of him that he ordered his three disciples to study with him.

Considering I knew my friend's *Sifu* was real enough to have killed opponents in personal empty-hand combat challenges in the 1930s in China, I thought I should check out this new *Sifu*.

I did; and even though he could only speak two words of English, "Yes" and "No," I decided to ask his permission to study Taijiquan with him.

Now here is the very strange part:

Tanemura *Sensei* had given me permission to study a different art with an instructor he never met based on what his low kyu level student told him.

This is not very common. In fact, it is extremely rare.

I went on to become this *Sifu's* disciple; and he and Tanemura *Sensei* became great Martial Art friends during their first meeting.

Just before Tanemura *Soke's* first New York *Taikai* after he had given me his permission to study with *Sifu* Chen, Tanemura *Sensei* told me he wanted to meet him when he was in New York.

Sifu Chen was honored; and said he would cook lunch for my Japanese *Sensei.*

By the way, *Sifu* Chen was an excellent cook; and we had a wonderful eight (a fortuitous number) course lunch.

After we had all eaten much too much delicious Chinese food, Tanemura *Sensei* began to ask *Sifu* Chen many questions about the history of *Gung Fu* and *Qigong* in China and the origins of some martial art techniques.

At that time, Tanemura *Soke's* English was not very good and *Sifu* Chen's was terrible. So they both asked me to try to make the other one understand what they were saying.

It wasn't going as good as Tanemura *Soke* wanted it to; and then Soke had a brilliant idea.

He began to write his questions in *Kanji*, using the oldest form of each Kanji he knew. *Sifu* Chen replied with Chinese characters and they continued to hand papers back and forth to each other for about two hours straight.

After each point was understood between themselves, one or both of them they shared what they had "discussed" with the rest of us.

To this day, I remember one of the questions and its answer:

Tanemura *Sensei* asked why the Chinese used one handed swords, when two handed swords were much more powerful.

Sifu Chen agreed with the statement about two handed swords being more powerful. However, he said the Chinese were willing to sacrifice some of the power for more speed and mobility.

Let's return to my first *Honbu* training trip again so that I can share a few stories with you.

My first trip to *Honbu* involved more than a dozen students. The group rented several vans; and, since I was the only one in the group who had experience driving on the left side of the road, I was delegated to be one of the designated drivers.

Tanemura *Soke* took us on excursions to the Buddhist temple and shopping for swords in Asakusa and to the famous temple and park at Nikko. So I did plenty of driving.

Everything was going fine, until we existed off of the highway on the way home from Nikko. I turned into the middle lane on the right side of the road. Thank God, I turned into a red light where I stopped and waited.

After I had stopped for the light, I looked across the intersection and saw three giant trucks lined up exactly opposite me on the other side of the street.

At that moment, I felt what a matador must feel if he is caught in the ring without his cape by an angry bull that is staring him right in the eyes at close range.

I must say no matter how good my movements had been during practice at *Honbu*, nothing was faster than me rocketing that van across the two far lanes and onto the left side of the road where I belonged. Interestingly, no one in the van saw my mistake. Only those reading this book know how close we came to misfortune that day.

I had been to the temple at Nikko in Japan twice before our trip with Tanemura *Soke*.

So I wasn't expecting this trip to be anything special. However, this trip turned out to be my favorite one because Tanemura *Soke* actually took the time to explain to us many of the details and much of the history of the site.

Of course, we went to the museum specifically to admire the antique swords on display there. I remember *Soke* joking about his "Wish List" and telling us which swords were number 1, 2 and 3 on his list.

On the way home, one member of our group broke out in hives due to an allergic reaction to something he had eaten on the trip. As soon as we returned to *Honbu*, Tanemura *Soke* immediately took him to the emergency room and stayed there with him for four hours until they sent the student home with Soke.

The next story is the only one I will relate that I am not telling first hand. However, enough people have told me their first hand versions that I believe it is accurate.

Even though this was 1990, I was almost forty years old. So I was passed the time when staying out all night sounded good to me. However, our group had several young men who were eager to experience the night clubs of Roppongi, Tokyo.

Like most major metropolitan public transportation systems, the Tokyo rail and bus systems shut down shortly after midnight. This meant if this group left for Tokyo after *Honbu* evening training, they had no chance of returning until the trains and buses started running again the next morning.

They had no problem with that. As soon as we returned home from evening training, they all showered, got dressed up and left for a night of partying in Tokyo.

So early the next morning (5 or 6 AM), they were all hurrying home to get ready for morning training (10 am) at *Honbu*. Even they were tired after partying the whole night long after two training sessions the day before, so they were kind of dozing off while riding on the train returning home.

One of my friends, who is a big, blond American was standing across the whole isle of the train with one hand stuck through the handles on each side of the corridor.

All of a sudden, a small, old Japanese man who had been sitting quietly in the front of the car stood up, screamed *Bonsai!* and then charged down the corridor straight at my friend.

My friend snaps suddenly awake; and finds his hands were stuck in the soft leather straps and he couldn't pull them free. So he starts to panic and struggles to get them out.

As the old man closes the distance, he gets ready to kick this charging crazy man. With his hands still stuck in the straps, my friend chambers his leg for the kick; and just before the man gets into kicking range, he suddenly stops, turns around and walks away laughing.

Everyone who was there teased my friend about this for the rest of the trip; and each time we all had a good laugh.

During this trip to *Honbu*, Tanemura *Soke* also took all of us down to Asakusa to see the famous *Sensoji* (*Kannon*) Buddhist temple and to shop at a small sword shop where he knew the owner.

We all bought the style of *iaito* (metal Japanese practice sword) which was being used by students at *Honbu* at that time... except me.

Somehow, I was the last person on line and when they got to me, they had run out of that style of *iaito* in my size. So I was given the choice of a less expensive *iaito* or a more expensive one. I reluctantly picked the more expensive one (a $100 USD more).

When we got to *Honbu*, Tanemura *Soke* asked to see my *iaito*. Upon examining it, he said I made a good choice. My more expensive blade had a more "real" feel than the others.

That made me feel better about spending the extra $100 USD. This *iaito* is now showing its age; but, twenty-three years later I am still using it.

Several years later, I asked Tanemura *Sensei* if he could find me a high quality *iaito*. He said yes; and added I must wait while he researched and waited for the right one for me to appear.

It took several months and then *Sensei* told me he would have several for me to look at when I came to *Honbu* the next month.

One evening after *Bikenjutsu* (secret sword fighting techniques) class at *Honbu, Sensei* told me to wait while he gathered and brought over several *iaitos* for me to look at.

Of course, everyone who was at class waited to see what *Sensei* would bring for me to look at.

When he returned with about six or seven *iaitos, Sensei* said he would not tell me anything until I had looked at all of the *iaitos* on my own.

I spent some time with each of them; however, I kept returning to examine one in particular.

When I was done, I said to *Sensei,* "I think they are all very nice; but, this one is my clearly favorite."

He said: "Ah. That is my favorite too. So there is no need for me to tell you anything."

I then asked *Sensei* its price; and he told me.

It was more than I had wanted to spend; but, I liked it a lot. So I asked *Sensei* "Can I think about it tonight; and let you know tomorrow morning"?

Sensei looked right through me and said: "Maybe I won't want to sell it to you tomorrow morning."

Everybody in the dojo laughed; and so that night I bought a very good *iaito.*

I remember *Sensei* told me as he was wrapping it up for me, "Generally, *katanas* (the most common type of Japanese swords) have a *scia* (scabbard) and *tsuba* (hand guard) to match the quality of the blade itself. This *iaito* has the *scia* and *tsuba* of a good quality *katana*. This iaito is very unusual high quality."

I have been told this *iaito* is worth twice the amount I paid for it. This is still my favorite and most often used *iaito*.

❀

If you are not aware of it, there is absolutely no doubting Tanemura *Sensei* has a great sense of humor.

Let me share with you these two examples of his wit which I remember from my early days in the Genbukan:

After the private night training session before a New York *Taikai* in the early 1990's, we were all eating out at a diner. *Soke* had ordered a lobster. One of the organizers had told the waiter to make sure it was a large one. And it certainly was.

The lobster arrived whole; and it was larger than the platter it came on. The waiter placed the platter down in front of *Soke*, and *Soke's* eyes widened when he saw it close up. *Soke* looked at it with his head tilted first one way, then the other way. We could see he was trying to figure out how to "attack" it.

All of a sudden he grabbed one claw and as he ripped it off he said: *Omote Kote Gyaku* (the Japanese name term for an outside wrist lock). Then ripped the other one off and said *Ura Kote Gyaku* (the Japanese term for an inside wrist lock).

Since all of us at the table were Jujutsu practitioners who had spent a good part of that day learning how to perform those same wrist locks exactly as Tanemura *Soke* wanted them done, we thought his joke was hysterical. The whole table laughed until many of us were crying.

One of my favorite stories about Tanemura *Sensei* is one of my more personal ones.

One Saturday evening in January in the late 1990s at Honbu, it was very cold, windy and snowing.

Due to the nasty weather, there were only two students who braved the weather that evening: myself and one of my *Senpais* (*Senpai* means senior student).

At one point in the training when it was my turn to be the *uke* (the training partner who receives the technique), my *senpai* asked me if I could take the *ukemi* (break fall) for a *Tomoe Nage* (a throw in which the *tori* or doer of the technique rolls to supine on the floor and sends the <u>uke</u> flying through the air to land hard on his back).

I said yes; and so we began the technique.

During this style of throwing technique, the *uke* can spend what-seems-like-forever floating upside down through the air before landing hard on his back.

Usually, the *uke* lands so hard on the *tatami* mats it makes a loud *boom*. And so it was with me……

Except, this time when I landed on the mats, there were two loud *booms* that filled up the whole dojo.

The first one was the expected one from my back slamming hard into the mats. The second one was the noise I made when I passed gas upon hitting the mats as hard as I did.

I was shocked, surprised and embarrassed.

I was lying on my back upside down looking at my partner who was also upside down looking back at me. He was clearly waiting for me to do or say something.

Just then, Tanemura *Sensei,* who was in the far corner of the room staying warm next to the portable heater, walked over to the space between myself and my *senpai.*

He tilted his head up and sniffed the air.

Then he said: "Ahhh, Secret Ninja Weapon"

and walked back to the heater.

We all laughed very hard for a very long time.

When we were finally ready to begin again, we grabbed each other; and just as we started to move, Tanemura *Sensei* suddenly shouted: *Yamete* or Stop.

Then he left the heater once more, walked to the dojo entrance and stepped one leg through the doorway out of the room and said:

"Just in case."

Needless to say, once again it took some time before the laughter stopped and we were ready to begin again.

Chapter 4:
A Turning Point

One could say that I am personally responsible for ending this beginning phase of The Tiger's Rise in the USA because I was responsible for ending his relationship with my former instructor, who was the organizer for most of the USA *Taikais* during those years.

Even though it may look that way on from the outside, it is not the complete truth. It makes my part in this Turning Point more important than it really is.

For several very good reasons, I did not want to continue studying under my former instructor. I believe he had changed in a way that was not right for me. I felt it was necessary for me move on.

That was when I decided to take advantage of a curious offer I remembered receiving a year or two earlier from Tanemura *Soke*.

In 1991 or 19992, during a *pre-Taikai* lunch I attended in Los Angles with many of Tanemura *Soke's* top students at that time, Tanemura *Soke* looked at me (the lowest ranking person at the table) and said: "I want you to open a Genbukan Dojo."

I was shocked; and said I was not in a position to do so at this time. Perhaps in the future I could.

Soke smiled at me and said he was patient and would wait for me.

I thought *Soke* was just being polite when he said he would wait. At that time, I had no idea I would be hoping his offer would still be open about two years later.

Yet, in 19993, two years after receiving Tanemura *Soke's* invitation to open a Genbukan Dojo, I asked his permission to open a Genbukan dojo.

He agreed; and because it was springtime; he named my dojo, *Harukaze,* or Spring Wind.

However, I felt the name was also given to me because at that exact point in time, my martial arts path needed a brisk wind of fresh energy at my back to help carry me forward.

The name *Harukaze* still inspires me.

My being accepted as a personal student by Tanemura Soke was used by my former instructor as one of the reasons he left the Genbukan and the KJJR. The rest of the details are not mine to share.

However, let me say I believe the reasons which prompted me to choose the Genbukan are the same ones which prompted my former instructor to leave it.

All the details which led up to my decision are other pieces of my Genbukan Path that I still do know much about. I will probably never know if they were planned by Tanemura *Soke* or if they were simply a part of our co-mingled fate.

For example, sometime near the end of the Los Angles *Taikai* and after I had declined Tanemura Sensei's request to open a Genbukan Dojo, Tanemura *Sensei* could see that Roy Ron *Shihan* (the *Taikai* organizer) and I got along well with each other.

Having noticed this, Tanemura *Sensei* asked Ron *Shihan* if he would "take care of me."

This means *Sensei* asked him to teach me as if I were Ron *Shihan's* direct student.

He agreed; and I began to travel once a month from New York to Los Angles for a weekend of private training with Ron *Shihan*.

This continued for about 18 months until I had reached my *Shodan* in Taijutsu and my *Shodan* in Bikenjutsu. It ended when Ron *Shihan* left Los Angles.

After that, I continued to train with Ron *Shihan*. However, I saw him much less frequently. We got together only when he had time to come to New York.

This training was very unique for someone outside of *Honbu*. Ron *Shihan* taught me as he had been taught when he was learning at *Honbu* during the very early years of the Genbukan.

This means I received older variations of Genbukan and KJJR *wazas* (techniques) than most of my contemporaries did.

It also meant my training was very hard.

My test for *Taijutsu Shodan* was 1.5 hours long; and, I was the only one testing. Ron *Shihan* divided the test in four parts. The first part was the one which is generally considered the complete test.

My Nidan test lasted for two hours straight.

My test for *Sandan* was "short"....only 45 minutes long because Ron *Shihan* had injured his back a few days earlier. This forced him to end this test earlier.

Simultaneously with the training under Ron *Shihan*, since I had experienced for myself the value of training directly with Tanemura *Sensei* as often as possible, I continued to attend every *Taikai* in the world up until a financial setback in the early 2000's left me temporarily unable to do so.

For the next few years after that, I was forced to pick and choose which *Taikais* I could attend.

Here is a lesson I learned at an early Belgium *Taikai*.

Tanemura *Soke* took us out to a park with a lot of forested areas for night training.

We learned and practiced how to hide in shadows, how to choose and how to climb trees.

Tanemura *Soke* also demonstrated how to run using *Happo Tenchi Tobi* on a long dirt road. In my mind's eye, I can still see Soke bounding down that dirt road as fast a jack-rabbit.

But, what made the most impression on me occurred when we were told to practice knife fighting at night in the forested area.

After a few minutes of practice, Tanemura *Soke* ordered us to stop so he could give us a big correction.

Soke said we were all using the techniques he had showed us; but, none of us were using the natural features of the forest to our advantage.

He said what made a Ninja so good at defense was that he used Everything to his advantage.

He then told us to try again.

This time, I maneuvered my opponent so that a small, thin tree was between the two of us. I then grabbed the tree and pushed it toward my opponent. Of course, he did a defensive maneuver to avoid the tree. As he did, I stepped in and won the contest.

Except of course, you can clearly see that I didn't win it. Tanemura *Soke* won it through me.

It was at the pre and/or *post-Taikai* instructor trainings that I honed my patterns in-between my trips to *Honbu* in Japan.

Tanemura Sensei got to know me a little better; and I began to slowly hold The Tiger's Tail a little bit closer to The Tiger himself.

The training and even just listening to Tanemura *Soke* words at these *Taikais* were like all-too-scarce rain falling on a parched desert. They would always inspire me to try harder.

The training at the early *Taikais* consisted of a lot of *Kihon* with some Goshinjutsu based on these *Kihons*. This help lay the foundation for my advancement.

Just like a desert would burst into bloom with new flowers after every rain, my martial arts practice would be re-energized and inspired for months after each *Taikai*.

48

I remember at another Belgium *Taikai*, Tanemura *Soke* had us practice an *Uchi-Mawashi Keri* (inside circular kick) as a defense against a round house kick to the thigh. Being at least twenty years younger, my partner and I practiced at full battle speed.

My partner was a European Kickboxing champion and he tried with all of his skill to get through. But, Tanemura *Soke's* technique stopped all of his attacks dead in their tracks.

At another Belgium *Taikai*, we were all at a restaurant for a post-training dinner, and Tanemura *Soke* spontaneously started to speak about how we need balance in our lives.

I was sitting about three or four tables away thinking about how valuable and special these personal times with Tanemura Soke were. So I raised my hand; and when *Soke* acknowledged me, I said to him, "I could listen to you speak all night."

And so it remains to this day.

Although I was almost always the only American at those early European *Taikais*, I was always amazed at how many people would travel from all over Europe to train with Tanemura *Soke*.

How can I say that when I traveled much further than they did?

I came because I wanted to become more like Tanemura *Soke*. In order to do so, I knew I had to train with him as much as often as possible.

Many of those who came to those early *Taikais* came to study the martial art of Ninjutsu itself with a Grandmaster. Interestingly, those who continued to study Ninpo in the Genbukan, realized in order to get as good as they wanted to get, they had to become more like Tanemura *Soke.*

Isn't it funny? No matter which of these goals a student wants, the path is The Same!

The fact that I invested so much of my life into my training has made me the person I am today. I understand This Path is not possible for everyone; so do not think I am recommending it for everyone.

My point is:

The amount you invest in training with The Right *Sensei* will produce changes in you which are greater than your investment. It is like buying a stock that is guaranteed to double in value.

Perhaps you think I am only basing this upon myself. Kindly rest assured I am not.

On the one hand, I can see how attending all of these *Taikais* has helped me progress much faster than if I had not attended them.

On the other, I can see how those who have moved to Japan and train regularly at *Honbu* have progressed at an unbelievably much faster rate than anyone else.

As an example, let me point out that I have trained with the *Shihans* many years before they were at the level of *Shihan.* By the time I met them in the late 1980s, they were already very good Martial Artists.

Now, they are simply better Martial Artists than I ever imagined a student could become. I am not limiting this to what they can do "on the mat." I truly mean they live their lives in a way I, as a Martial Artist, aspire to do.

They are so much like their *Sensei* (Tanemura *Soke*) that I am always amazed when they spontaneously say something that reminds me of Tanemura *Soke.*

They are proof positive that if you want to become like your *Sensei,* you must earn his trust through your actions. The more your *Sensei* trusts you, the more comfortable he will feel about sharing his *Kudens* (a Sensei's personal teachings) with you.

Of course, we cannot leave the early years without mentioning the creation of the Panther video series.

At that time, Panther was probably the largest and most influential producer of Martial Art videos in the world. They invited Tanemura *Soke* to make one series of videos; and were so impressed with his Martial Talent and Spirit that they ended up making several video series.

They then proceeded to prominently feature these videos and Tanemura *Soke's* name in all of the major martial art magazines of the time.

Chapter 5:
The Middle Years

By this time, the Tanemura Soke's explosive techniques on the Panther videos had worked their magic. They brought a good deal of interest and new members to the Genbukan and KJJR.

Tanemura *Soke* was starting to be featured on TV in Japan and internationally. His Genbukan Taijutsu and KJJR *Jujutsu* manuals were now the standard textbooks for Ninjutsu practitioners around the world regardless of what organization they belonged to.

His Genbukan, KJJR, weapons and *ryuha* (unique, individual Styles of Japanese martial arts) videos, first in VHS, later on CD Rom and now on DVD were and are still sold to Martial Artists all over the world.

Also at this time, a lot of the initial enmity between the various Ninjutsu organizations was being to wane. Thus, none questioned Tanemura Soke's physical abilities, his martial skills and his talent to teach others how to perform those martial skills at levels unmatched anywhere else

His almost Super Human Martial Spirit was also recognized and admired by all.

This period was also very important because it marked the time when Tanemura *Soke* as 58th Grandmaster of the *Amatsu Tatara Bumon* (Martial teachings) and *Shumon* (Spiritual teachings) also began in earnest to introduce its ancient (approximately 2700 years old) teachings of to all of the members of the Genbukan.

For those of you who are not familiar with the teaching of Amatsu Tatara, here are some of its core tenets:

- The Universe and Everything in it, including us, are connected to The Creator.

- There is an Order and a Purpose for Everything in Creation.

- It is our Duty to learn what Our Purpose in this life is; for we are all born with or for a Purpose.

- It is difficult to learn our True Purpose because our egos get in our way.

- It is our duty to accomplish our mission in this life. It is why we were born.

- We all have Guardian Spirits who watch over us and help us as much as we allow them to.

- The Creator has made available to us all the help we need.

Part of this help is our *Sensei*. Things will be a lot easier for us if we choose the *Sensei* we are supposed to choose.

Interestingly, a few years ago when Tanemura Sensei and I were discussing the path I have taken in This Life, he told me we have had the same instructor-student relationship in several previous lives in several different countries in several various arts including Yoga, Qigong and Chinese Martial Arts.

Wow, what a powerful statement.

It says many things.

But, perhaps the two most important are Tanemura *Sensei* is telling me our fates are intertwined.

And, since we have kept our *Sensei – Deshi* relationship across these lives, there is something I must learn before I can leave The Wheel of Life; and Tanemura *Sensei* is the person who is destined to help me learn it.

Tanemura *Soke* began to introduce the teachings of Amatsu Tatara slowly. He knew true understanding of the basic concepts could not been rushed.

He wanted his students to have enough time to realize if they did not accept the Spiritual Teachings of the Shumon, he would not think less of them as students in the Bumon (Martial Arts).

It was and is Tanemura Soke's mission to teach us.

It was and is our responsibility to accept them or not.

Tanemura *Soke* will fulfill his mission. He left it up to us to fulfill our duties as we saw them.

Sometime in the late 1990's, the Genbukan began to evolve into its next phase of development. This was when Tanemura *Soke* decided the time was right for him to tighten the enforcement of the Genbukan rules and regulations.

More specifically, Tanemura *Soke* felt it was now time to let all of his students decide if they were willing to become students of a *Koryu Soke.*

Up until this time, Tanemura *Soke* was working hard to show the world he could deliver what he promised. Now, he felt he had succeeded; and only those who were biased would question his status. Thus, it was now his students' responsibility to acknowledge him appropriately for what he undoubtedly was:

A legitimate *Soke* of True *Koryu* Japanese Martial Arts.

Those students who left his organizations at this time were those students who were not able to accept the role of a *Koryu Deshi.*

That's right. I am coining a new phrase, *Koryu Deshi* or traditional student.

Usually, the Japanese word *Koryu* refers to Traditional Japanese Martial Arts because the word translates as *Old School.*

Therefore, when I use the phrase *Koryu Student,* I am referring to a student who believes in the same values as a student in a traditional Japanese Dojo would believe and who would act in the same way as that student would.

Remember the old saying:

"You get what you pay for"?

Well, in a *Koryu* Dojo the currency is Respect, Honor, Loyalty and Obedience.

Offer Respect, Honor, Loyalty and Obedience freely in a *Koryu* Dojo and the student will receive in True *Koryu* Teaching more than he "paid for."

Now, it was time for the members of the Genbukan to offer Tanemura *Soke* his due in full measure of Respect, Honor, Loyalty and Obedience.

It was not the way of a *Koryu* student to tell his *Sensei* what he wanted to learn, when he wanted to learn it and when he was ready to test for it.

The second New York *Shibucho* had difficulty accepting this point. By not accepting his role as a *Koryu Deshi* and continuing to push hard against the wishes of his *Sensei*, Tanemura *Soke*, he had backed himself into a corner.

When his plans for himself failed to materialize as he wanted them to, he left the organization.

Shortly, thereafter, he had convinced another important USA member that it would be in his best interest to leave and join with him.

Recently, I was discussing this book with Michael Coleman *Kyoshi*, who has been a personal student of Tanemura Soke even longer than I. He shared with me a story he was witness to that fits in perfectly right here at this point in the story:

A student asked Tanemura *Soke* how long it would take him to reach his next level in rank. Soke answered him. Then the student replied he did not want to wait that long.

Tanemura *Soke* simply said to him: "If you want to go faster, which part do you want to skip"?

Let me continue the tale:

These two high ranked students left because they felt they knew what was best for them. Obviously if you know what is best, if anyone disagrees with you, they must be wrong.

So it was right for them to leave their *Koryu Sensei* because they were not able to commit to being a *Koryu Deshi*.

Another high ranked student left shortly thereafter when I was made *Shibucho* of New York because he thought that honor was his.

Once again, here was a student who thought he knew the best decision for his *Sensei* to make for his organization. It was fitting that these three like-minded students joined together after leaving the Genbukan.

One of the key points to understand is what it means to "Trust" someone's judgment.

We only need to "Trust" someone's judgment when their view of something does not match our own.

There is no need to "Trust" someone's judgment when they agree with you.

Again, I ask: Why would someone pick a *Sensei* to show them Their Path if they believe they already know Their Path better than their *Sensei?*

A few years after these incidents, a few high ranking students left the Genbukan because they did not understand another key point of being a *Koryu* Student:

For all practical purposes, there is very little (if any) difference between a *Koryu Soke* and his organization(s).

Indeed, one could accurately say, the *Soke* of a *Koryu* organization Is that organization.

An organization is defined by its rules. One can even say an organization is it rules.

So when one member of an organization expects a different set of rules to apply to himself or herself, they are not actually asking for the rules to be changed.

Because changing the rules is changing the organization, they are really asking to be allowed to belong to a different organization.

Further, if the *Soke* of an organization is that organization; when you ask to change the organization, you are asking the *Soke* to change.

I hope this makes it sound as crazy to you as it does to me.

Of course, Tanemura *Soke* could not change himself, his organizations and their rules just to suit a student's personal desires.

And so it was, these students chose to leave the organization when *Soke* made it clear he could not make special rules for certain individuals.

Can it be a coincidence that to the best of my knowledge none of these dropped-out students has ever become the personal student of another *Sensei?*

Can it be they do not need another *Sensei?*

Maybe.

However, considering the fact that even Tanemura *Soke* has a *Sensei,* perhaps the answer to this question lies somewhere else.

Perhaps the breaking of the Heart-to-Heart bonds with a *Koryu Sensei* for the wrong reasons can change The Heart of the person breaking those bonds.

Tanemura *Soke* has said:

"The Heart of a Spiritual Warrior is most important. The Heart is deeply involved with all *Koryu* Arts."

Therefore, the higher a person's advancement (rank) in a *Koryu* Art the more their Heart is involved.

The more their Heart is involved, the greater the change will be if they break the Heart's bonds for the wrong reasons.

If a person's Heart changes, then they have changed.

If their Heart has changed for the better, than they have changed for the better. If their Heart has changed for the worse, then they have changed for the worse.

Tanemura *Soke* has taught more on this subject.

He has also said:

"Any dropped out person, especially if high level, loses their connection with this art, the heart of these *Koryu* arts and their connection with its *Soke*.

Not only do they lose this connection, but the Genbukan level they had drops down.

***Koryu* arts deeply involve the heart.**

When the heart connection is broken, previous ability is altered.

The true martial art level is lowered.

This is a deeper point."

Can you hear the Ringing of Certain Truths when you read this Kuden?

I do.

Let me end this section with another *Kuden* I received from Tanemura *Sensei* at a *Taikai* in the early 2000s.

When we were traveling by car for sightseeing, I mentioned to Tanemura *Sensei* I was working on my legs and feet: How to make my *kamaes* (fighting stances) strong and rooted all of the time.

Sensei turned to me and simply said:

"That is the beginning of Mastership."

During the mid-1990's, Michael Coleman *Kyoshi* expanded the size and scope of his Milwaukee *Taikais*.

They became a cornerstone of Genbukan training with Tanemura *Soke* outside of *Honbu;* and continue to do so whenever Tanemura *Soke* comes to the USA.

At one of the Milwaukee *Taikai's*, I was accompanying Tanemura *Soke* up to his room. And I related this story to him.

Sensei, Outside of my kitchen window in New York, I have a stone statue of a Thai style Buddha who has a small, half-smile on his face.

He and I are good friends and I "visit" with him every time I sit down to eat. I am always amazed he can wear that smile all of the time.

One day in the middle of winter, it was very, very cold and snowing very hard when I sat down to eat. I looked out the window to see

The Buddha; and there he was sitting with that same smile on his face even though he was covered with snow and ice.

Just as I was about to ask him how can you still be smiling, I heard your voice (Soke's) in my head say one of your favorite sayings:

"Because It doesn't matter."

Tanemura *Sensei* replied: "Ah, you are very fortunate to understand this. You had a small *satori* (a moment of partial Enlightenment)."

Although the *Taikais* at each of the main *Taikai* locations: Belgium and the UK, Milwaukee and New York were all Genbukan and KJJR *Taikais*, Tanemura *Soke* gave each area's teachings a different flavor.

Even though every *Taikai* at that time offered all of the same Genbukan and KJJR material, it seemed to me the European *Taikais* generally did more physical practice of the *Kihon*, Milwaukee seemed to focus more on the technical points of the *Kihon*, while New York seemed to offer more *Goshinjutsu* (self-defense) based upon the *Kihon*.

You can see that attending all of the *Taikais* is the best way to get as broad a scope of training as possible outside of living near *Honbu*.

All during this time, up until 2005, I continued to train at *Honbu* at least once a year and sometimes twice. I supplemented the regular *Honbu* training schedule with private lessons whenever Tanemura *Sensei* had the time.

This was the best plan I could put together for my training with Tanemura *Soke*.

At this point, I would like to recommend that if your Genbukan training is important to you, you must formulate a plan to maximize the resources you have available.

I know this may sound trite. But, many students' plan consists of telling themselves they will go to training whenever they can.

And while this approach is good up to a certain point, simply telling yourself you will take advantage of whatever opportunity presents itself is not much of a detailed, specific plan to maximize your training.

Another way of describing this plan is: If you are lucky, you will be able to train more rather than less.

This kind of thinking ignores one of my favorite sayings:

"A Good man (or woman) makes his own luck."

Therefore, a student needs to set aside as much time, money and energy (of course, energy: if you have the time and money for training but no energy left, how much good can the training do for you?) as their life permits.

If you never realized it, some of the best students in the Genbukan (three of the *Shihans*) decided to change their lives dramatically (by moving permanently to Japan) in order to actualize their personal plans to optimize their training in the Genbukan.

Of course, this is not appropriate for everyone; but, the point is You need to have a plan which matches the importance of Your training.

Let me lighten the mood a bit by sharing my third sword story.

As you now know, every one of my Japanese blades comes with a unique story behind it. It is as if I was fated to own each and every one.

At the end of the 1990's, I asked Tanemura *Sensei* if he could find me a nice *Shinken* (a true Japanese sword). He said yes; but, again he said I must wait for a while he researched and waited for the right one to appear.

After one year or so, *Sensei* told me I was in luck. He had found what he though was the perfect *katana* for me.

When I next went to *Honbu, Sensei* showed me a wonderful sword with a great story behind it.

He had obtained a *katana* that was made especially for a Japanese sword master in the same year I was born in. However, he had died unexpectedly shortly after receiving the sword; and thus, had never used it.

His family had kept it unused for about fifty years. They let Tanemura *Sensei* have it only because they knew him personally.

This turn of events ended up much better than either of us hoped for. The sword was literally a perfect fit for me.

This meant, although it's blade was shaped like a *katana's,* it was actually long enough to be officially classified as a *tachi* (a longer style of sword than the much more common *katana*) which was unusual.

It was fitted with a greenish *scia* (also very unusual).

All in all, my *Sensei* found a sword for me which seemed as if he had it custom made for me at a discounted price.

Each of the swords my *Sensei* found for me was special in some unique way; and, each new one was more special and unusual than the preceding one.

It was as if the deeper our fates became entwined with each other, the more strongly special things were drawn to us to help the both of us accomplish our purposes.

In 2005, Tanemura *Soke* held the first Genbukan World *Taikai* in Japan.

I believe the fact that over three hundred members from all six continents attended this event heralds the Genbukan's coming of age.

Tanemura *Soke* had already shown the world he is all he claims to be. However, the world still needed some time to respond to this fact.

The 2005 Genbukan World *Taikai* was the world's overwhelming response to The Rise of Tanemura *Soke* and his Genbukan World Ninpo Bugei Federation.

Here ends the Middle Years of The Tiger's Rise.

Chapter 6:
The Current Plan

I called this chapter the current plan and not the final plan.

Why?

Because knowing Tanemura *Sensei* as I do, I am sure nothing is acceptable as *The Best.*

No matter how good something may be, Tanemura *Soke* will always strive to improve it.

I deliberately did not say "strive for more."

Why?

Because more is not always better.

Only Better is Better; and sometimes less of something is better.

If "more" truly meant "better," than we would not need the word "better."

Once a student asked Tanemura *Soke* when will he stop changing things.

Soke replied: "After I die."

Over the coming years, Tanemura *Soke* will do whatever he can (and in some cases, whatever he must do) to refine and enhance his organizations.

The good news for his students is:

In order for Tanemura *Soke* to refine and enhance his organizations; he must refine and enhance his students!

Tanemura *Soke's* current plan contains probably the greatest changes I have seen in his organizations.

Why do I say this?

Because Tanemura *Soke* has evolved on All levels of his being.

He is more patient with his students' mistakes and shortcomings on some levels and stricter on other levels.

If you know *Soke* well enough, you can actually see his patience at work as a calmness washes across his face as he bears some of our mistakes.

Last year, I witnessed a mistake made by a student of *Renshi* level. Tanemura *Soke* wanted to give him a *Kuden* (direct personal teaching) by demonstrating a technique on him.

To accomplish this, the student had to grab *Soke* in a certain manner. But, things were a little more complicated than usual because the student had to "attack" the throat of his partner (*Soke*) to begin this technique.

The complication is one of respect: one should never attack one's *Sensei* with such a dangerous action. It is impolite at best; and at worst, it can be construed as an attack and responded to appropriately.

I know that in the early years, a person doing this to Tanemura *Soke* would have ended up in great pain after the first "attack." If the student did it again, he might have ended up incapacitated (with something damaged).

In this instance, *Soke* simply kept hurting the offending body part of the student each time he repeated his mistake. *Soke* knew the student did not understand *Soke's* response as a rebuke to stop "attacking my throat" and thought *Soke* was just demonstrating a different self-defense technique.

I was watching this firsthand; and I was not sure if I should have enlightened my friend.

However, after about ten "attacks" ending with the exact same moderately painful response by Tanemura *Soke* and the student "dutifully" accepting *Soke's* response; but not understanding its meaning, *Soke* actually explained to him what he did not understand.

Needless to say, on the next attempt, the student corrected his mistake; and modified his attack making it appropriate for his *Sensei* and his *Soke*.

Compare that to my own story which took place almost twenty years earlier when I was at a *Bikenjutsu* class at *Honbu*.

At this class, Tanemura *Sensei* decided to practice sparring with all of us.

When it was my turn to spar with *Sensei*, I had not been told that a *deshi* does not "spar' with his *Sensei*. The *Deshi* simply learned whatever it was his Sensei wanted to teach him at that time.

So because I was not expected to attack my *Sensei,* when I suddenly did, I was lucky enough to hit his wrist (as you will see, "unlucky" is much more accurate description).

Sensei acknowledged the point I scored. We stopped; and took our beginning positions again.

Sensei started the next round by feinting his *shinai* (bamboo practice sword) upwards and I responded by following his Ki (internal energy) up with my *shinai*. Then *Sensei* exploded downwards and hit me with his *shinai* first on one side of my body, then on the other, again and again and again until I was huddled into a ball against the back wall.

When Tanemura *Sensei* was finished "teaching" me my lesson, I took some time to recover and acknowledged the point with a bow and *Arigato Gozaimasu.* We then bowed to each other and switched partners.

Both my friend and I learned our lesson from Tanemura Soke. However, just as Soke had changed, so did the manner of our teachings.

Just as Tanemura *Soke* is now less strict in some instances (as you have just read), he is definitely stricter in others.

He has become a little more accepting of non-Japanese manners from those who do not know better but whose heart is good.

On the other hand, now that many of the Genbukan members hold higher ranks and titles, *Soke* is holding more members to higher standards of Japanese manners which befit their status, especially if he knows they have already been made aware of them.

Therefore, behavior and thinking which might be acceptable from a lower ranked person might not be accepted from a higher ranked person.

Indeed, the higher rank person would be expected to not even think like a lower rank person.

Of course, the best would be if a higher rank person no longer held the same beliefs as he or she did when they held lower ranks.

This is one of the reasons why, generally speaking, the higher the rank, the longer the time between advancement.

In today's society, earning a higher rank in a true, complete Martial Art should mean more than learning new *wazas* or techniques.

It should mean you have also progressed as a Spiritual Warrior (Tanemura *Soke's* term).

What does this mean?

If a person uses the term Spiritual Warrior, it must mean they believe in a spiritual realm (for Tanemura *Soke*, this Spiritual Realm is Heaven or the Realm where God's Will or Plan is performed by All who reside there). Like any realm, a Spiritual Realm must have its own rules.

A warrior is a person who is committed to do battle (not necessarily physical battle) in order to uphold The Principles he or she believes in.

Therefore, a Spiritual Warrior on this earth is a person who is committed to enabling Heaven's Way to unfold here on earth as it is in Heaven.

Each rank in a Japanese Martial Art should mean you, as a person, Are that rank: you Feel, Think, Speak and Act as a person of that rank should.

Taijutsu (*Jujutsu*, etc.) is only one part of a rank.

In the words of Michael Coleman, *Kyoshi*:

"The higher your rank in the Genbukan, the better equipped you are to serve people of lower rank (those who need help)."

A good *Sensei* will ensure that his students evolve as people and not just progress as warriors.

In other words, he will ensure that you are a True Martial Artist and not just someone who does Martial Arts.

If you only want to learn just a particular Martial Art, what will you do if you lack the physical gifts to be as good as you hoped to be?

What will you do as you get older and can't perform as quickly and powerfully as you once did?

However, if what you want is to learn how to be the kind of person your *Sensei* is in every way, then those two issues will not be as overwhelmingly important to you.

Now in 2014, Tanemura *Soke* is respected all over the world as one of the greatest living Martial Artists.

He knows this because it is a fact and not out of ego conceit.

In 2012, Tanemura *Soke* held the *Gikan Ryu Koppo Jutsu World Taikai* in Japan.

This was a very special Martial Art event because up until then, *Gikan Ryu* was one of those very special, completely secret Martial Arts which most martial artists only dream about learning from a legitimate master instructor.

In the months prior to the *Taikai,* Tanemura *Soke* released his *Gikan Ryu* videos for the world to see.

A short time before their release, I was at *Honbu* for training. *Sensei* and I were discussing *Gikan Ryu*: the upcoming videos and the Taikai.

He told me these events would shake up the Martial Art's World because *Gikan Ryu* contains the highest levels of *Ninpo Ryuha.*

Soke explained it was part of his mission to share the Highest Levels of Martial Arts with his students.

And *Soke* was more correct than I imagined.

This was not only because it was *Gikan Ryu,* but because it was Shoto Tanemura *Soke* demonstrating *Gikan Ryu Tanemura Ha.*

Tanemura *Soke* has also been raising up the level of his organizations; which means he has been raising up his students and Dojo-chos.

Tanemura *Soke* has done this by teaching us how to be True *Koryu* students.

That's correct.

I believe teaching us *Koryu* Martial Arts techniques needed to wait until we became more like *Koryu* students (true traditional *Deshi*).

If we want to see exactly what *Koryu* Martial Arts Students look and act like, all we have to do is watch and learn from the Genbukan *Shihan-Kai* (the group consisting of All the Genbukan *Shihans*).

We have a long way to go; but, obviously Tanemura *Soke* thinks we are close enough so that:

Tanemura *Soke* has begun his True Mission:

To make The World a Better Place to Live In by teaching his students Truths which have never been taught openly by anyone before him.

This is why he is now teaching *Amatsu Tatara* more openly and completely to more people than ever before.

Why is this something special?

As its Grandmaster, only Tanemura *Soke* holds the complete knowledge of *Amatsu Tatara Shumon and Bumon.*

"*Amatsu* means Heaven or Nature. *Tatara* means the highest secret teaching system of Martial Arts and original Shintoism Spirit.

Only he can accomplish this task.

Preserving these ancient teachings and traditions is a great responsibility which requires great personal sacrifices on the part of the teacher. Understanding this point is only possible if one can understand the teachings themselves

This special knowledge is contained in the *Amatsu Tatara Hibumi,* "which are special, secret scrolls about Koryu Martial Arts, Spiritualism and Humanism." (from Genbukan.org)

Does this mean Tanemura *Soke* doesn't think Martial Arts are as important as he used to?

ABSOLUTELY Not!!

This is why *Soke* is now openly teaching various *Ryuha* (Martial Arts of a specific school or lineage) for the first time.

However, in order to understand how a Martial Art fits into Heaven's Law, once needs to understand Heaven's Law.

In the words of Tanemura *Soke*:

"The True Heart of Ninpo is the *Amatsu Tatara*: Bumon (the martial side) and Shumon (the spiritual side) are completely and inextricably combined."

Learning the True meaning of a Martial Art without understanding Heaven's Way can lead to the improper use of that Martial Art: using it against Heaven's Law either knowingly or even unknowingly.

Indeed, one can say that a High Level *Sensei* will teach a Martial Art to a student only up to the level that student understands Heaven's Way.

If you believe this, then you should be already packing your bags to attend the 2015 Takamagahara World *Taikai* at which time Tanemura *Soke* will reveal some of the deeper Truths of *Amatsu Tatara Shumon* (Spiritual World) and *Bumon* (Martial World).

Through his own personal training, Tanemura *Sensei* has opened His Awareness to receive knowledge from more than his five senses.

This is a rare very talent.

Not because more people do not have the ability to do so. Rather, it is because most people do not know how to use the ability they have. Actually, it is more likely true they do not even know they have this ability.

This *Taikai* will be a chance to see and understand the fruits of a lifetime (many lifetimes for those that believe in the re-birth of souls).

This Is Exactly Why You have chosen to follow a *Koryu Soke* of a *Koryu* Martial Art.

Now, let's return to my 2013 Japan trip for one last time.

As I related earlier, at the beginning of our first lunch, Tanemura *Sensei* said he would test me for *Nanadan Jujutsu* the next time I came to *Honbu*, which would be the following year.

A few days later, I was in *Honbu* for self-training. It was very hot (actually, Japan was setting a record heat wave during my stay). Not surprisingly, I was the only person in the dojo and was training by myself.

I was sitting in seiza, studying my notes when Tanemura *Sensei* parted the *Noren* (Doorway Curtains) at the back of the dojo and said to me "It is very hot today. Take care and drink more water."

I said *"Hai, Sensei"* or Yes, Sir.

Then he added as if it was nothing extraordinary:

"I will test you for *Naginata Jutsu Shoden* and *Jujutsu Nanadan* before you leave."

I said *"Hai, Sensei; Domo Arigato Gozaimasu"* or Yes, sir. Thank you very much.

Interestingly, almost immediately after that, a problem developed which no one could have foreseen; and for which Tanemura *Sensei* asked me for my help.

We spent many hours working together. As a courtesy, Tanemura *Soke* took me to lunch and then to dinner afterwards. At the dinner, it was fairly late; and we were relaxed and pleased with the success of our work.

Sensei said to me:

"It is very strange. As soon as I said I would test you for *Nanadan*, you have a new chance to help the Genbukan. Thank you for your efforts."

I replied, "It is my duty as your student, so it is no problem at all."

This is a very important point:

When you accept an honor, the duty that comes with that honor cannot be viewed as a hardship.

Can we say breathing in order to stay alive is a hardship?

No, because it is part of being alive.

It is almost as if it is not something we do to stay alive, it is something that is a part of being alive.

And so it is with being a *Koryu* student of a Koryu *Sensei*. Your duty is as much a part of being a student as breathing is a part of being alive.

Then I politely asked Tanemura *Sensei* why he changed his mind about testing me.

He looked right at me and without hesitation said:

"Because Heaven told me to."

Very interestingly, this keeps a very odd fact of my Genbukan path intact:

Since my *Sandan* (3rd Degree Black Belt), unlike perhaps every other senior student, I have tested for the next level of *Jujutsu* before the next level of *Taijutsu.*

Why?

Maybe I will find out the next time I see my Sensei.

And maybe I won't.

Permit me to step aside as a Genbukan *Kyoshi* for one moment, and look at this event as a person.

Why?

Because I think I can be objective about Tanemura *Soke's* achievements and status.

I cannot tell you how being asked to take this test and be accepted by this person whom I truly hold in awe makes me feel.

As I type these words, it is now more than ten months since I was told I was to be tested (yes, I was not asked if I wanted to test) and almost as long since I passed my test. Yet, I still almost cannot believe it.

It is an honor I had wished for; but, one whose importance did not really hit me until the moment it happened.

So regardless of what I thought, I must admit I was not prepared for it beforehand.

How can you prepare for something you did not understand before it happened?

Kindly let me return to my role of *deshi*.

Still to this day and for at least the last twenty years, as part of my morning spiritual ablutions and prayers, I say:

"*Sensei,* Thank you for the knowledge you have given me."

義鑑流世界大会2012
玄武館本部

Why?

First, I do it out of respect for the person (Tanemura *Sensei*) himself.

Second, I do it out of respect for the knowledge he has given me.

It helps remind me that All I know does not belong to me.

It is not mine to change as I see fit or to keep hidden beyond the rules I must follow.

Every morning I also say:

"Dear *Amaterasu Omi Kami*, Please let my Heart Shine like The Sun."

Most people are familiar with the Lunar Zodiac and its twelve year cycle (the twelve animals, as I related earlier in this book). However, most do not know the complete cycle is not twelve years; but sixty years.

There are five cycles of twelve years; one for each of the five elements.

When a person reaches their sixtieth year, the cycle begins again. It is known as your *Red Egg Year* in Chinese Astrology and is very auspicious time.

It is a time for endings and new beginnings.

I have now passed my sixty third year.

Therefore, let me share some knowledge with you I have learned the hard way (by living it):

Do not waste any time.

Pursue that which is important to you.

I most certainly intend to attend the 2015 Japan *Taikai* and hope to see all of you there.

I would like to end this book with a personal entreaty to all of you:

Make The Universe Noble!

Chapter 7:
2014 Update

I have recently returned from my annual training at Honbu.

This year I met three Dojo-chos from Spain and one of their students. We became good friends and traveled together several times including a trip to Kawagoe city (whose old section still looks like 19th century Edo or Tokyo).

There are three stories from this trip to Honbu I would like to share with you.

All of the foreign students visiting Honbu in July 2014 arrived on the same day. Therefore, it was convenient for Tanemura *Soke* to take all of us out for our welcome lunch at the same time.

Lunch was at a very nice Italian restaurant. All of the visiting students and Tanemura Soke sat at the same table.

After our starter of soup, we all ate pizzas and pastas family style with shared dishes (*Soke* made sure there was more than enough vegetarian food for me).

We ate and talked for about two hours.

While we were all in the car returning back to our apartments, I told Tanemura Soke about something strange which happened to me at training a few nights before.

It was at the evening training the day after I arrived. Due to jet lag, I was tired even before class began.

Therefore, when we were sitting in Mukso (meditating while sitting in seiza) at the beginning of class, I asked the Spirits of Honbu Dojo to please give me the strength to train safely and well.

Just as I said that to myself, a bolt of energy shot up my spine so that I actually shivered a little.

After that, I felt refreshed and trained well for the whole class.

Sensei turned back to look at me and said: "Because you asked with a pure heart; and because your Heaven's Gate is already opened, you were able to receive that gift from Honbu."

Believe it or not, hearing those words from someone whose Spiritual development I hold in the highest regard was one of the most powerful moments of this trip.

The second story details a mistake I made that was so serious I was reprimanded for it three different times.

This is a perfect example of Tanemura *Soke* holding his higher ranked students to high levels of traditional Japanese manners.

At Saturday training, there was to be a test for *Renshi* (beginning level of mastership) at *Honbu.* Even though I had an arthroscopic knee surgery in April and my knee was still slightly swollen, I felt I could sit in *seiza* through it all without any problem.

And I did.

However, just before the testing began, Tanemura *Soke* asked another student to test for *Nidan Taijutsu.* At that point, I did not want to jump up and make a big deal about my knee.

The test took a lot longer than I thought it would and about two-thirds of the way through, my knee began to swell up and hurt a lot. I withstood the pain for some time; but eventually I began to feel as if I was damaging my knee because I felt it swelling up. So I slipped out of *seiza* into a cross-legged position.

I was immediately corrected and told by a Shihan to return into *seiza.*

Then after the test, Tanemura *Soke* (who did know about my knee) came over and corrected me again with very strong words in front of everyone.

A few days later during private training, again Tanemura *Sensei* admonished me for moving out of *seiza.* Since we were alone, I mentioned about my knee swelling because of the operation.

Sensei said: "Yes, I know about your operation. But, you did not mention it to me at test time. So everyone who was there thought you simply decided for yourself not to sit in *seiza* anymore.

That was very bad Japanese manners. Had you asked me before the test, of course I would have given you permission to break *seiza*."

I would like to end on a more pleasant note.

I spent the whole month of July 2014 working on two Ryuhas: *Chugoku Kenpo* and *Asayama Ichiden Ryu Menkyo Kaiden*.

I learned much more than I hoped for. I had never focused for so long on just two *Ryuhas* before.

I wished the month would not end.

About the Author

Gary Giamboi has been studying martial arts since 1969.

He began studying with his present with Sensei, Shoto Tanemura in 1988. He became a member of the Genbukan World Ninpo federation in 1990 and the Kokusai Jujutsu Renmei in 1991.

He is also a published author, Qigong practitioner, Yogi, a National Academy of Sports Medicine certified personal trainer, founder and owner of the Genbukan Harukaze Dojo, The Institute of Asian Arts™ and Training by Gary.

He has been studying the Eastern Arts since 1969 has attained many ranks and titles along the way including:

• Kyoshi and Shibu-Cho in the Genbukan World Ninpo Bugei Federation

• Ryokudan in the Genbukan World Ninpo Bugei Federation

• Nanadan in the Kokusai Jujutsu Renmei

• Okuden in Assayama Ichiden Ryu Taijutsu in the Genbukan World Ninpo Bugei Federation

• Chuden in BIkenjutsu in the Genbukan World Ninpo Bugei Federation

- Shoden in Bojutsu in the Genbukan World Ninpo Bugei Federation

- Shoden in Naginata Jutsu in the Genbukan World Ninpo Bugei Federation

- Nidan in Hanbo Jutsu in the Genbukan World Ninpo Bugei Federation

- Takagi Yoshin Ryu Shodan Mokuroku

- Shoden Menkyo in Gyokko Ryu in the Genbukan World Ninpo Bugei Federation

- Shoden Menkyo in Shinden Tatara Ryu in the Genbukan World Ninpo Bugei Federation

- Shoden Menkyo in Koto Ryu in the Genbukan World Ninpo Bugei Federation

- Shoden Menkyo in Shinden Fudo Ryu in the Genbukan World Ninpo Bugei Federation

- Shoden Menkyo in Kijin Chousui Ryu in the Genbukan World Ninpo Bugei Federation

- Nikyu in Chugoku Kenpo

- Menkyo Kaiden (Mastership) in Taijiquan and Qigong in the Taishan Guangdong Chen Wei Gun Wushu Federation

- Level 4 (Master Level) in Qigong from the National Qigong Association of the United States

- Recognized by Yogiraj Swami Bua Ji as an instructor of his system of Hatha Yoga and Hindu Wrestling Exercises including Indian clubs and Rope Yoga

- E-500RYT Yoga instructor from the Yoga Alliance

- Level 2 instructor in Thai Yoga from Jonas Westring

- Certified Practioner of Ohashiatsu (Shiatsu) from the Oshashi Institute

- National Academy of Sports Medicine Certified Personal Trainer

- Pilates Mat and Reformer instructor certified by June Kahn

- Nidan in Goshin Jutsu from Robert Hansen

- Shodan in Tae Kwon Do from grandmaster Suh Kahn Kang

Gary believes in working with the Universal Principles which are the basis of all true religions, modalities and systems.

These Principles may not be easy to learn, accept and follow, but they are simple.

They usually require seekers to give up more than actually acquire. This is true for many reasons, not the least of which is most people already know all they need to know even if they can't "see" it or admit it if they can "see" it.

His first book, *The Spirit of Smiling: Perfecting the Art of Surrendering to The Way* has received many very positive reviews from martial artists, Yogis and Qigong practitioners.

He has produced several DVDs on Qigong and two on Yoga (produced in Japan by Grandmaster Shoto Tanemura) and a relaxation CD which are available on Amazon.

www.ingramcontent.com/pod-product-compliance
Lightning Source LLC
Chambersburg PA
CBHW060553100426
42742CB00013B/2540